Beat P. Truffer

The History of the Matterhorn

The History of the Matterhorn

First Ascents, Projects and Adventures

by Beat P. Truffer

(Translation by Mirjam Steinmann)

2. Up-to-date edition

———— Aroleit-Verlag ————

To the Mountain Guides of Zermatt

The author would like to express his gratitute to:

Bruno Jelk, Zermatt
Swiss Alpine Museum, Berne
Mountain Guide Centre, Cervinia
The Cantonal Library of Valais in Sion
Swiss Alpine Club, Section Zermatt

And to all others who assisted in the gathering of information and thus made possible the publication of this book.

First Edition 1990
2. Revised, up-to-date edition 1992
Copyright 1990 by Aroleit-Verlag
Aroleit-Verlag, Haus Saphir, CH-3920 Zermatt
All rights reserved.

Translated from the German book:
Die Geschichte des Matterhorns

Cover Picture: Beat P. Truffer
Photographs: Beat H. Perren, Swiss Alpine Museum, Beat P. Truffer
Printed by: NBV Druck AG, Visp – Printed in Switzerland

ISBN 3-905097-07-9

TABLE OF CONTENTS

Part I

THE FIRST ASCENT

Previous Events

In the middle of the 19th century Zermatt was a small, cut-off mountain village whose inhabitants lived almost exclusively on their own agricultural products. They often had to contend with merciless hunger.

In those days only very few people visited Zermatt, these being mostly scientists. The only guesthouse in the village had just three beds and was run by the village doctor. A small mule-track was the only connection from Zermatt to the valley of Visp. At that time the Matterhorn was of no great importance as it was considered unscalable. The summit was said to be haunted by ghosts.

With the awakening interest in high Alpine climbing, every year the number of visitors to Zermatt increased. Most of the adventurous tourists came from England. Already at the end of 1854 there were three guesthouses with a total of 67 beds.

Famous mountains like the Montblanc (1786) and the Jungfrau (1811) had been climbed long before the mountains around Zermatt became an object of interest to the ambitious alpinists. In 1855, the highest point of the Monte-Rosa-Massif, the «Dufour-spitze», was conquered by mountaineers. In the same year the industrial magnate from Alsace, Dollfuss, had the idea of climbing the Matterhorn with the help of an air-balloon, but he was not able to realize his plan.

Two years later, in 1857, the first attempt to ascend the Matterhorn was made. In the following years, 18 expeditions resulted in failure before the first ascent was accomplished. Most of the attempts had been made from the Italian side. In eight expeditions Jean-Antoine Carrel and Edward Whymper took part, sometimes together, sometimes in separate teams (see «The Chronicles of the Matterhorn»).

In the meantime all the other high mountains of Zermatt had been climbed. Only the Matterhorn remained invincible.
Just as the Bastille in Paris had been stormed on 14th July 1789, so the rock fortress of the Matterhorn was to be conquered on the same date in the year 1865.

The Struggle for Victory

On 7th July 1865 Edward Whymper comes to Valtournanche. He persuades Jean-Antoine Carrel to a further attempt to climb the Matterhorn. But the weather is bad. Due to other commitments Carrel cancels the arrangement with Whymper after three days.

On 11th July at daybreak, while Whymper is still asleep, Carrel sets out with a few men from Breuil towards the Matterhorn. Whymper is indignant. He wants to go to Zermatt, but there is neither a guide nor a porter to be found. Towards midday Lord Francis Douglas, together with Joseph Taugwalder, a son of Peter Taugwalder, arrives at the small Italian village of Breuil. After a short talk with Douglas, Whymper comes to know about his project to climb the Matterhorn. They join forces and traverse the Theodul Pass. The weather is no better.

As soon as they arrive at Zermatt they search for Peter Taugwalder senior and persuade him to an ascent of the Matterhorn. On the way to the Monte Rosa Hotel, Whymper runs into Michel Croz, a guide with whom he had already undertaken several other ascents. At that moment Croz is employed by the clergyman Charles Hudson and the young Robert Douglas Hadow. As both Englishmen and Croz are envisaging an ascent of the Matterhorn, they decide to tackle the mountain together.

The next morning at half past five — it is Thursday 13th July — the party sets out. The sky is cloudless. Eight men (Peter Taugwalder senior, two of his sons, Croz, Whymper, Douglas, Hudson and Hadow) walk up via the Schwarzsee to the base of the Matterhorn.

On a protruding plateau at the starting-point of the mountain, which lies a little above the present day Hörnli Hut, they set up a tent bivouac (10,640 ft). In the afternoon Croz and Peter Taugwalder son reconnoiter the lower part of the mountain.

Meanwhile the Italian party has reached the height of 13,000 ft on the Lion Ridge (South-East Ridge) under the leadership of Carrel. There they install their night camp.

Before dawn Whymper and his six friends pack up their equipment and in the first light of day they start the climb over the Hörnli Ridge (North-East Ridge). In the meantime Joseph Taugwalder returns to Zermatt. On the east side of the mountain the men are making quite good pace. Later they change over to the ridge for a short time and climb higher. Then they continue over the snow-covered «shoulder». They take two breaks. After the second break, Croz takes over the leadership, Whymper and Hudson having taken turns with each other up till now. A little more to the right they tackle the real, technically more difficult climb to the summit.

After quite a time, one by one they reach the peak on the Zermatt side. The weather is favourable. Fruitless searching for footprints assures them: the Matterhorn is theirs! With this the eight-year struggle for the pioneering ascent comes to an end.

Croz and Whymper discover the Italians about 720 feet below the summit. The Italian team had only advanced slowly. When Carrel realizes that Whymper has been the victor, he turns back.

The Accident

After a long rest on the summit, they discuss the order in which they should descend. On the summit they leave behind a bottle containing a piece of paper carrying their names.

Croz is to be the leader on the way down. He is followed by Hadow, Hudson and Douglas. At the end we have Peter Taugwalder senior, Whymper and Peter Taugwalder son.

Soon they come to the lower part of the «Roof» of the mountain (as the formation of the summit is also called). This is not an easy section to master, as many fissures are filled with snow and ice and therefore don't offer many handholds. For safety reasons only one man moves at a time. When Croz is laying his ice-axe aside in order to help Hadow climb down, the latter slips and pulls Croz, Hudson and Douglas down into the depths. The rope between Douglas and Peter senior breaks. Both of the Taugwalders and Whymper are left alone, suffering from shock.

Quite a time goes by before the remaining three recover. In great fear they slowly climb down the Matterhorn. Very soon daylight fades and they see themselves obliged to spend the night at an altitude of about 13,400 ft.

After a long night they climb down to Zermatt with drawn faces and bring the sad news to the village. An atmosphere of deep grief spreads in Zermatt.

The next day at two o'clock in the morning — it is Sunday, 16th July — three British mountain companions, two Frenchmen and three guides set out with Whymper from Zermatt to search for the victims. The mountain guides of Zermatt cannot take part in this search, as they would be excommunicated by the priest for having neglected the morning mass.

The searchparty discovers three bodies on the Matterhorn Glacier; those of Croz, Hudson and Hadow. As for Douglas — only a few of his belongings are found.

Three days later 21 mountain guides recover the bodies and bring them to Zermatt. Hadow and Hudson are buried on the north side of the Catholic cemetery and Croz in the centre. Lord Douglas' body, however, has never been found.

After Hudson had lain in the old cemetry of Zermatt for 46 years, his remains were transferred to the English Church of Zermatt. Today two graves which commemorate the two Englishmen Hudson and Hadow (upper terrace, next to the steps) as well as a memorial stone for Croz can be found in the Catholic cemetry of Zermatt.
A few clothes, the broken rope and further belongings of the victims are exhibited in the Alpine Museum of Zermatt.

Bird's eye view of the summit (photograph: Beat H. Perren)

The Persons Involved

1. The Survivors

Peter Taugwalder Senior (also known as Geppi) 1820—1888

«Old Peter» was born in Zermatt in 1820. He had made his name thanks to several ascents of the Monte Rosa and was known to be one of the best mountain guides of his time. In 1841 he married Anna Maria Zumtaugwald who bore him four children.

One week before he tackled the pioneering ascent of the Matterhorn, he climbed the Coeur Ridge on the Obergabelhorn for the first time, together with F. Douglas and J. Vianin. Taugwalder was known to be taciturn, harsh and strong.
The court case that followed the first ascent (see «The Consequences») destroyed Taugwalder's reputation as a mountain guide. He left for America. A few years later he returned to his native village. He died there in 1888 near the Schwarzsee, probably as a consequence of appendicitis.

Peter Taugwalder Son 1843—1923

«Young Peter» had only just turned 22 at the time of the pioneering ascent of the Matterhorn. He was Taugwalder senior's eldest son and married twice (1867 and 1878). In 1871, six years after the tragedy on the Matterhorn, he undertook his second ascent of the Matterhorn. Up until an accident in the nineties which made climbing impossible for him, he climbed the Matterhorn about 120 times. He was silent and reserved. As he knew the Matterhorn so well, he was nicknamed «The Matterhorn Peter».

When his life drew to an end he retired to his property «zum Biel» (a place between Täsch and Zermatt). He died at the age of eighty years on 9th March 1923.

Edward Whymper 1840—1911

In order to sketch some of the mountain peaks, the draughtsman, copperplate engraver and later also author Whymper visited the Alps for the first time in 1860, scarcely 20 years old. In the following years he succeeded in numerous first ascents, such as the Grandes Jorasses, the Aiguille Verte, the Grand Cornier and the Ruinette. After eight failures, Whymper also achieved the summit of the Matterhorn. He was described as cold and calculating. After the accident he went to Greenland and later to the Andes. In 1874 he climbed the Matterhorn a second time.
In the Alps he visited Zermatt and Chamonix regularly without, however, making any extravagant climbing expeditions. He died of a heart attack on 9th September 1911 in Chamonix.

Peter Taugwalder senior and junior's grave in the cemetry of Zermatt (upper terrace, third row on the right)

2. The Victims

Michel Auguste Croz 1830—1865

Croz was known as one of the best mountain guides of his time. He came from Chamonix and had made many important first ascents. Everyone admired his strength and fearlessness. Apart from being a shoemaker, he devoted his whole life to the mountains which, in the end, cost him his life.
For the French his death meant a great loss.

Reverend Charles Hudson 1828—1865

Beside Peter Taugwalder Senior, the vicar of Skillington, Lincolnshire, at the time 37 years old, was the oldest participant of the pioneering ascent of the Matterhorn. He was popular, devout and well-liked. His remarkable climbing skills brought him fame as a first class mountaineer.
In the twelve years preceding the first ascent of the Matterhorn, he had undertaken several different, extremely demanding ascents.
On 5th July 1865 he climbed the Moine Ridge of the Aiguille Verte together with Croz.

Robert D. Hadow 1846—1865

1865 was the first year of Hadow's career as a mountaineer. On 9th July he had climbed the Montblanc in very little time, accompanied by Hudson. Although he was very tough and a quick walker, he lacked experience in mountaineering. This came to light above all during the descent on the Matterhorn when he showed signs of anxiety and insecurity when encountered with a difficult passage. The tragedy of the first ascent started with the slip of this young man.

Lord Francis Douglas 1847—1865

With 18 years he was the youngest of all Matterhorn pioneers. This man proved to be exceptionally strong-willed. He had undertaken several tours with Taugwalder senior; at the end the pioneering ascent of the Obergabelhorn.

This list would be incomplete without a mention of J.A. Carrel. He was the driving power behind a great many attempts on the Matterhorn.

Jean-Antoine Carrel 1829—1890

Born in 1829 in Valtournanche, the mountain guide Carrel grew up in very simple conditions. His biggest goal was to make the first ascent of the Matterhorn from the Italian side. He was considered to be a very good rock climber — Whymper's greatest rival. No fewer than eight times did he make attempts on the mountain, until in the end Whymper beat him. It was only three days after the Englishman's victory that Carrel reached the summit of the Matterhorn from the Italian side.
On 26th September 1890, the guide died of complete exhaustion at the foot of the mountain. With his last ounce of strength Carrel had led his guests safely down the Matterhorn after a sudden change for the worse in the weather.

The Consequences

1. The Hearing

The first climbers of the Matterhorn had been tied together with three ropes for the descent. The first stretched from Croz to Douglas, the second from Douglas to Taugwalder senior and the third from Taugwalder senior to Taugwalder son. The middle rope proved to be the weakest, and soon after the accident rumours arose that Whymper or Taugwalder senior had cut the rope.

After the tragedy of this first ascent the government of Valais instituted an investigation committee. The members were as follows: Joseph Anton Clemenz, investigating judge from Visp; César Clemenz, deputy referee; Donat Andenmatten, secretary from Visp and as usher ad hoc Jean Julen from Zermatt.

For three days, one after another, Whymper, Taugwalder senior and two guides who had taken part in the search for the victims were questioned and Taugwalder senior was questioned a second time.

The court came to the conclusion that no criminal act could be proved by the facts provided, and that Hadow was responsible for the accident. Upon this, the case was dismissed.

Although Peter Taugwalder senior was also found innocent through this, the accusations did not by any means cease. His whole life he suffered through them and he felt rejected by other people.

A copy of the minutes of the case can be seen in the Alpine Museum of Zermatt.

2. The Press

The news concerning the dramatic happenings of the first ascent of the Matterhorn caused a big wave of excitement in the press; in Switzerland, as much as abroad. The most affected were the English. Their grief gave way to indignation. In the English press whole articles appeared on the sense and non-sense of mountain climbing. The whole world over newspapers reported the tragedy on the Matterhorn. No other Alpine event has ever caused more headlines.

Even Queen Victoria of England went into the matter of the fatal accident. After a talk with the Lord Chamberlain, however, she decided not to take legal measures that would forbid mountaineering to all Englishmen.

Zermatt with the Matterhorn became world-renowned in no time at all. Its name was on every tongue. This event may be seen to have been the beginning of the development of Zermatt into a world-famous resort.

Part II

THE OTHER RIDGES AND THE FACES

The Lion Ridge (also known as the Italian Ridge)

Only three days after the tragedy on the Matterhorn, people were standing again on this 14,687 foot-high mountain. The victory belonged this time to Jean-Antoine Carrel and Jean-Baptiste Bich.

After Carrel had had to come to terms with the fact that Whymper had been the faster of the two on that 14th July 1865, he returned to Breuil with his men without continuing the ascent. The inhabitants of the valley of Valtournanche were dismayed at the news of their defeat, as they had thought that their men had reached the top first.
The same day — it was 15th July — a new group of daring men, encouraged by a patriotic engineer, joined forces in order to attempt the climb from the Italian side for the first time.
On 16th July, in the morning after a service in the church of Breuil, the four men Jean-Antoine Carrel, Jean-Baptiste Bich, Abbé Gorret and J. Augustin Meynet set out on their Matterhorn-expedition. They made their way up to the Col du Lion (a depression between the Matterhorn and the Tête de Lion) and further up the ridge to the foot of a great pinnacle where they fixed up their bivouac.
The next day they advanced to the place where Tyndall had broken off his pioneering attempt three years ago. From this point nobody had ever climbed higher on this ridge. Carrel suggested going round the mountain peak from the west, as there was no chance of succeeding on the South-West Ridge. Rock and ice-fall, however, soon forced them to change over to the right of the ridge.

The south side with the Pic Tyndall (left)

Just underneath the summit, after crossing a strongly inclined rock-slip, Gorret and Meynet remained behind in order to facilitate the way back for the others. Carrel and Bich tackled the last few metres without their companions and were able to shake hands in victory.

This ridge was climbed in winter for the first time — after two previous attempts — by Vittorio Sella and a few other men on 17th March 1882.

The Zmutt Ridge (North-West Ridge)

Since the pioneering ascent of the Matterhorn, talk about the mountain had somewhat died down. However, two virgin ridges and four faces still remained temptingly unapproached.

The Englishman Alfred Frederick Mummery was preparing his expedition to the Zmutt Ridge with his guides Alexander Burgener and Augustin Gentinetta in Zermatt, when they got the message that another party had already set out with the same goal.

All the same Mummery and his guides made their way towards the Staffelalp. On the Zmutt Glacier the other party with William Penhall and the guides Alois Zurbriggen and Ferdinand Imseng came towards them. The weather seemed about to change, so Penhall's guides decided to turn back. Mummery, however, insisted on continuing to the hut on the Stockje.

As surmised, the weather changed for the worse. Burgener and Mummery sent Gentinetta to Zermatt in order to get supplies and an extra guide. In the meantime they set off to reach the foot of the Matterhorn. In the evening they met Gentinetta and a guide from Saas, Petrus Johann, and they set up a bivouac.

Contrary to all expectations the morning of the 3rd September 1879 produced a crystal clear sky. At the beginning the footprints of their predecessors, who had had to give up because of a sudden change in the weather, enabled them to make quick headway.

After the «Zmutt-Teeth» (Zmuttzähne) the mountain guides, faced with a difficult passage, hesitated to go on. Then they heard the other roped party which was also on the mountain again. The race for the laurels of the Zmutt Ridge was about to begin.

While Mummery and his men climbed back to the ridge after a traverse, Penhall and his guides were scaling a good part of the West Face. Mummery's group was the first to reach the summit over a strip of rock, known today as the Carrel-Gallery, (Carrel used this traverse during the pioneering ascent of the Lion Ridge). The others had gone wrong and lost precious time. 75 minutes later Penhall's group was also standing on the peak of the Matterhorn.

On 25th March 1948, in excellent winter weather conditions, the mountain guide Eddy Petrig from Zermatt scaled the Zmutt Ridge with his guest Henri Masson from Paris. They started out from the Hörnli Hut at 5 a.m. and reached the top at 2.15 p.m. Who actually made the first ascent of this ridge in winter (before the beginning of spring) is not known.

The Matterhorn with the Breithorn (left), from left to right: Hörnli Ridge — Zmutt Ridge — Lion Ridge

The Furggen Ridge (South-East Ridge)

Just one year after the successful ascent of the Zmutt Ridge (1879), Mummery was in Zermatt again. This time, together with Burgener, he wanted to tackle the last of the four great ridges, the Furggen Ridge. At the level of the Furggen Shoulder they weren't able to get any further on this shortest, but at the same time also most difficult ridge of the Matterhorn, so they crossed the East Face under difficult conditions to get to the Hörnli Ridge.

The next try on the Furggen Ridge was made in 1890 by the well-known alpinist and author Guido Rey. Within a space of eight days he attacked this ridge three times. Three times he failed.

Nine years later Guido Rey returned to the South-East Ridge. A little above the Furggen Shoulder a 650 foot-long rope which was anchored to the summit was thrown to him and his companions by several hired men. Although they were able to climb several feet higher with the help of this rope, they had to abandon the attempt just before the summit. The Furggen Ridge seemed invincible.

Not until 1911 was the notorious South-East Ridge again tried by alpinists. At the second attempt Mario Piacenza reached the top together with Jean Joseph Carrel and Joseph Gaspard on 9th September by keeping to the right and thus by-passing the incline southwards to the summit.

In 1930 Enzo Benedetti, Luigi Carrel and Maurice Bich climbed the Matterhorn on the left of the incline up to the summit. At last, on 23rd September 1941, the last part of the Furggen Ridge was scaled directly. The party included Luigi Carrel, Alfred Perino and Giacomo Chiara. In order to master this difficult incline they used 43 pitons. Since the first attempt in 1880, 61 years had gone by, until the complete scaling of the Furggen Ridge could be accomplished.

The first to climb the upper part of the Furggen Ridge in wintry conditions by by-passing the overhangs were J.Fuchs and R.Monney. From the Solvay Hut they crossed the East Face and arrived at the top by going over the Furggen Shoulder on 28th March 1948.

The Furggen Shoulder

The first completely successful scaling of this ridge in winter was carried out by the Italian mountain guide Walter Bonatti with his companion Roberto Bignami on 21st March 1953. In 1989 three Italians climbed the Matterhorn using the Piacenza-Route in winter for the first time on 10th February. (See «The Chronicles of the Matterhorn»).

The West Face

The West Face

The highest face of the Matterhorn (4,600 ft.) has up until now only rarely been attempted. During the competition of the Zmutt Ridge a major part of the West Face had been scaled by the Englishman William Penhall with his guides Alois Zurbriggen and Ferdinand Imseng from Saas in 1879.

The next ones were the well-known Austrians Lammer and Loria in 1887. But because the rock slabs further up were very icy, both of them turned back. On their way back they were struck by an avalanche and dragged down to the Tiefmatten Glacier. They only just escaped death.

42 years later a young man from Vienna called Fritz Herrmann walked up to the West Face. Even before he reached the Face he had lost his crampons. All the same he began to climb. With neither pitons nor rope, nor crampons, and equipped only with a worn-out ice-axe, he took up the hazardous enterprise. A little to the right of Penhall's route, he climbed up the face foot by foot. The higher he got, the more icy became the rock. Using all his strength, Herrmann gripped the smallest fissures with his fingers to escape the deadly fall. Suddenly an ice block gave way under his feet. But miraculously, his rucksack got stuck between two rocks and saved him from certain death.

After he had bivouacked on a little ledge without securing, he went on the next day. But he too crossed under the face of the summit to get on to the Zmutt Ridge.

But the ambition of the alpinists demanded a complete scaling of the West Face. Yet another roped party failed. Luigi Carrel and Carlo Taddei also had to give up on the Direttissima because of a sudden change in the weather.

In April 1949 the two Swiss Raymond Monney and Jean Fuchs made the assault on the West Face in winter, but the two had to own themselves beaten and go over to the Zmutt Ridge.

On 13th August 1962 the Italians Giovanni Ottin and Renato Daguin were the first to succeed in climbing to the top of the Matterhorn directly up the West Face. They bivouacked at the foot of the face and reached the summit of the Matterhorn before sunset of the same day. It was a remarkable performance.

The last face to be scaled in winter was the West Face in 1978. After a difficult three-day climb, seven Italians scaled the forbidding face on 11th January (see «The Chronicles of the Matterhorn»). In this group there were also three of the four climbers who had taken part in the pioneering ascent in winter of the South Face.
While they were climbing down, the mountain guide Rolando Albertini fell and was killed and another was injured by a rock fall. The survivors dedicated this pioneering ascent to their deceased friend Albertini.

The upper part of the West Face

The North Face

This 3,600 foot-high face of the Matterhorn is known to be one of the most difficult north faces of the Alps. Its ascent is a hazardous undertaking even for expert alpinists. The worst enemies for the climber are rock fall and sudden changes in the weather. Again and again this face appears in the headlines.

After all the ridges of the Matterhorn had been climbed, there seemed to be no more glory to be gained from this mountain. Then the forbidding North Face became more and more the centre of interest for the most ardent mountaineers. Three attempts failed in 1923, 1928 and 1930. (See «The Chronicles of the Matterhorn»).

In the summer of 1931 the two brothers Franz and Toni Schmid from Munich cycled from Germany to Zermatt. Their goal was the North Face of the Matterhorn.
On 31st July they started from the Hörnli Hut, crossed the Matterhorn Glacier and began the ascent of the extremely steep ice flank of the wall. The two brothers could rely only on the front spikes of their crampons and the securing ice-pitons. After the wall of ice they had to progress over the rock face of the mountain.
The snow and ice on the face began to melt when the sun's rays reached them. Owing to the wetness of the rock, they could only move slowly. All of a sudden Toni Schmid slipped. By a miracle, during the fall, he was able to catch hold of a small ledge and hang on to it. They were still more than 1,300 feet below the summit. At dusk they had to fix up an emergency bivouac on the face. At daylight, stiff with cold, they continued their upward climb. Icy slabs of rock increased the difficulty of the face. Only with the greatest efforts were they able to gain height. Gradually the face got less steep. They managed to get up to the Italian summit, although they were taken by surprise by a violent storm just below the summit. It was already past midday. They climbed down to the Solvay Hut and spent the next night there.

Bird's eye view of the North Face (photograph: Beat H. Perren)

For this brilliant performance in alpinism they were awarded a gold medal at the Olympic Games of 1932 in Los Angeles.

In July 1959 the Austrian Dieter Marchart climbed the face solo in the record time of five hours.
For the centenary celebration of the pioneering ascent of the Matterhorn, Yvette Vaucher was the first woman to succeed in scaling the North Face. She was accompanied by her husband and the mountain guide Othmar Kronig from Zermatt.

The North Face in Winter

After the scaling the Eiger North Face in winter, the north face of the Matterhorn became the main attraction again. During the winter months of 1961 and 1962 the face rejected five roped parties. Among the participants were well-known names such as Walter Bonatti and Toni Hiebeler (the latter was one of the pioneers of the winter ascent of the Eiger North Face).

On 2nd February 1962 eight mountaineers were in the Hörnli Hut: two Swiss, two Austrians and four Germans. All had the same goal: the north face of the Matterhorn. Outside the temperature was minus 20 degrees Centigrade.

The next day three teams made an assault on the face. The first to go were the Swiss Hilti von Allmen and Paul Etter. Soon afterwards followed Werner Bittner, Reiner Kauschke, Peter Siegert, Leo Schlömmer and Erich Kempke. Toni Hiebeler remained behind in the hut. On this day the Swiss reached an altitude of 13,612 feet. The other parties were about 330 feet lower. Although one of the Swiss lost his crampons in the night, and despite a violent snow storm, this team managed to reach the top the next day. Hilti von Allmen and Paul Etter had made it.
The second team did not progress so quickly and had to set up a second bivouac in the face. They reached their goal in a big storm, 22 hours after the Swiss.
The Matterhorn had yet another sensation to be talked about.

From the 18th—22nd February 1965 Walter Bonatti climbed the face solo, taking four days and at a temperature of minus 25 degrees Centigrade. The Italian guide set foot on the summit on 22nd February at 12 minutes past 3 p.m. He had found a new route which led farther right than the Schmid-Route through the North Face. With this, Bonatti had completed that route which Viktor Imboden and Kaspar Mooser had already begun in their attempt to climb the North Face with very modest equipment in 1928. This route was named after Bonatti.

The first woman to master the face in winter was the Japanese Akiko Shigi, on 9th March 1978, together with her husband. At the same time the first team of women were tackling the wintry North Face. One of these four Polish women was suffering from frostbite, and so the four women had to be rescued by a helicopter a little below the summit. Nevertheless, one of them maintained having reached the top.

Up to this day, neither the Japanese nor the Czechoslovakian route has ever been used in winter.

Bird's eye view of the South Face (photograph: Beat H. Perren)

The South Face

Since 1930 mountaineers had been pitting themselves against the 4430 foot-high south face of the Matterhorn. After the North Face had been climbed for the first time on 31st July/1st August 1931, the Italians wanted to keep the South Face for themselves. But the weather was unfortunate for a long time, since it was snowing quite far down in the valley.

On a fine day, 15th October 1931, the Milanese, Enzo Benedetti and the guides Luigi Carrel and Maurice Bich set off for the pioneering ascent of the South Face. Already on the lower part of the face they were repeatedly taken by surprise by falling stones. With the utmost care they climbed up rapidly. The perpetual rock fall turned the climb into a dangerous undertaking.

By and by the sunrays changed to shadow. Towards 4 p.m. the team was at the base of the «head» (highest part of the Matterhorn from the South). Considerable difficulties made the last few lengths of rope a time-consuming job. At 6 p.m. they tasted victory: the pioneering ascent of the South Face lay in their hands. It was getting dark quickly now and they climbed down slowly in the dark to the Solvay Hut.

But the South Face also has other interesting routes to offer. On the left side of the face there is a ridge that leads up to the Lion Ridge. This ridge was named after the Italian Ugo De Amicis. Together with Arrigo Frusta, De Amicis tried the ridge several times in 1906. Again and again he had to give up before the last section.

Three decades went by before three young men from Valtournanche decided to climb the De-Amicis-Ridge in 1933. Amilcare Crétier, Toni Gaspard and Basilio Olietti reached the Pic Tyndall via the last unconquered section. As they were climbing down the Italian Ridge they were struck by stones which sent them hurtling down into the depths.

Yet another ridge ends between the massif of the summit and the Pic Tyndall. Luigi Carrel and Albert Deffeyes established this new route in 1942.

At last the South South-East Face was conquered by Luigi Carrel, Abbé Louis Maquignaz and Italo Muzio on 3rd/4th September 1953. For the last 1,300 feet alone they used 60 pitons. This Muzio-Carrel-Route ends on the south-east point of the Furggen Shoulder. Since this ascent, the final point is called Pic Muzio. A more direct way up to the Pic Muzio was found by Annibale Zucchi and Giuseppe Lanfranconi on 11th—13th August 1965. Their route is said to be the most difficult on the south side of the Matterhorn.

On 22nd/23rd December 1971, the first scaling of the South Face in winter was recorded. This success was attributed to the brothers Arturo and Oreste Squinobal. One hour later Ettore Bich and Innocenzo Menabreaz also reached the top.
The mountain guides from Italy were active particularly in the eighties. In this decade no fewer than seven pioneering ascents in summer and in winter were performed successfully by them on the south side of the Matterhorn.

The East Face

The East Face

The last face to be attacked was the east face of the Matterhorn. Because of the danger of rock fall this face had been despised for a long time.

Once again Luigi Carrel, an expert mountain guide took part. Because he was so short, he was nick-named Carrelino. One cannot speak of the story of the mountain without mentioning the name of Jean Joseph Carrel's son in the same breath (pioneering ascent of the Furggen Ridge in 1911), for he was involved in the pioneering ascents of the South Face and that of the Furggen Ridge. Nobody has ever conquered as much virgin land as he did.

On 18th September 1932, only a year after the successful pioneering ascent of the South Face, six Italians left the Hörnli Hut early in the morning. Four of them were young guides. That morning they crossed over the Furggen Glacier in order to begin the climb of the 3300 foot-high rock wall in the centre. Carrelino led the first rope, to which Enzo Benedetti and Antonio Gaspard were tied. Then followed Maurice Bich, Giuseppe Mazzotti and Carrelino's brother, Lucien on another rope.

As soon as the sun rose and it became warmer, stones became loose and fell crashing down. With a great deal of luck the mountaineers were able to climb higher in the intervals between the volleys of falling rocks. Only once Bich was hit by a small stone. Things were going well again.

As early as 9.30 p.m. they were at the summit wall, the «head» of the mountain. For these last 820 feet they took 23 hours. The vertical, at places overhanging face of the peak was not so easy to master. The six alpinists spent the night clinging to the summit wall and made hardly any progress. In the night it snowed. All the same they reached the peak the next morning.

Just as the Alpine performance on the South Face had been, so in the same way, was that on the East Face overshadowed in the headlines by the previous North Face ascent. But this brilliant performance of the six men would not be repeated for a long time yet.

In 1953 a second attempt by the Italians ended in defeat. Only 27 years after the first ascent were men supposed to have mastered the entire East Face. Jan Mostowski and Stanislav Biel maintain having scaled the face in April. There is, however, no evidence to prove this.

The upper part of the East Face

On 26th/27th February 1975 the three mountain guides from the Valais, René Arnold, Guido Bumann and Candide Pralonge performed a real masterpiece. Under the leadership of Arnold they took the route of the pioneers and set up a bivouac at an altitude of 14,100 feet and at a temperature of about minus 10 degrees Centigrade. The next day at 13.45 p.m. they had completed the first ascent of the East Face in winter.

The North North-West Face and the Zmuttnose

Between the north and the west face there is yet another face. This is the North North-West Face which ends in the Zmuttnose. The two routes that lead over the Zmuttnose are the most difficult and up-to-date ones of the Matterhorn. Only a small number of even the world's best alpinists is capable of approaching the peak of the mountain by following these routes over the Zmuttnose. On 14th July 1969, exactly 104 years after the pioneering ascent of the Matterhorn, Leo Cerruti and Alessandro Gogna crossed the Matterhorn Glacier in order to get to the base of the North North-West Face. The major part of this ascent route is protected by the partly overhanging Zmuttnose, so that the risk of rock fall is nil. After they had passed the crevice of the mountain, the two Italians started their climb of the face below the Zmuttnose.

The mountaineers had to bivouac three times and they were not able to dispens entirely with artificial aids, such as pitons and wooden wedges. Above all the overhanging part of the Zmuttnose demanded an extreme effort from the men. After they had mastered the most difficult sections they climbed across the upper part of the North Face up to the Zmutt Ridge and reached the peak on 17th July.

Twelve years later two aspiring mountain guides found a more direct route over the Zmuttnose. On 28 July 1981, Michel Piola and Pierre-Alain Steiner spent the night in the Hörnli Hut. The next day at 3 a.m. they were on their way to an extraordinary ascent. Soon after the beginning of the climb, with rucksacks weighing 80 kg, they were to ascend an extremely steep ice face before they were able to continue on the rock.

The aspiring mountain guides came to the actual Zmuttnose on Friday, 31st July 1981. Even this exposed and very difficult passage was mastered by Piola and Steiner. One day later they had reached the top of the Matterhorn by taking a new route.

On 21st-28th January 1974, the Swiss Edgar Oberson and the Czechoslovakian Tomas Gross stood at the Zmuttnose. The pioneering winter ascent of the Zmuttnose via the Gogna-Route lasted a whole week. To the present day several of the ropes from this first ascent are still to be found on the route.

The famous mountain guide André Georges from the Valais was the first to use the Gogna-Route alone. After two days he set foot on the summit on 14th July 1982.

The first time the Piola-Steiner-Route was trodden in winter was on 26th-31st December 1982 by the mountain guides Daniel Anker and Thomas Wüschner. In March 1983 two Bulgarians spent 17 days on this route. After 16 bivouacs these mountaineers at last got to their goal. No ascent of the Matterhorn has ever taken so long.

The most difficult side

Part III
CHRISTIAN SYMBOLS, HUTS, PROJECTS AND LEGENDS

The Cross on the Summit

At the turn of the century the communities of Zermatt and Valtournanche decided to erect a Cross on the Summit of the Matterhorn. The Cross was manufactured within a short time in cast iron in Italy and covered with a protective coating so that it would withstand the rough climate. In the centre of the Cross was a silver medallion with a small Maltese Cross mounted on it. On the left arm of the Cross stands the name «Patrumbor» (the Latin name for Zermatt) and on the right one the name «Vallistornench» (the Latin name for Valtournanche).

At the beginning of the summer 1901, the Italians had dismantled the 9 foot-high and 90 kilo-heavy black iron Cross into several pieces and planned to carry it up the Matterhorn. But weatherwise that summer was unfortunate. The conditions in the mountains did not permit the undertaking.
It was only in September 1901 that twelve mountaineers from Valtournanche were able to set out in order to carry the heavy burden up to the summit. But they did not get far. At the altitude of 12,750 ft., near the refuge hut Luigi Amedeo di Savoia they had to give up their project because of a storm. Throughout the winter, the Cross for the Matterhorn was left lying in several pieces in the hut.

The next year several attempts had to be made before the iron Cross was at last able to be set up and anchored down on the Italian summit which lies a little lower than the Swiss summit of the mountain. The transport of the Cross was accomplished by Antoine, Battista, Daniel and Luigi Maquignaz, Jean-Jacques

Carrel, Luigi Pession and J.B. Pellissier. On 24th September 1902, Abbot Augusto Carrel read the first mass next to the Cross of the summit.

Since that year the sign of God stands above the gap in the ridge on the Italian summit (14,681 ft.). In order to protect the Cross from damage in storms, it is furnished with a lightning conductor.

At the beginning of 1965, three Italian mountain guides had to set the Cross up again after it had been thrown over in a storm. A few years ago the medallion in the middle of the Cross was unscrewed and taken away by some unknown people. Not even at this altitude do thieves hold back from such acts.

The Madonna on the Matterhorn

On 26th July 1951, Mrs. Hilde Erlanger traversed the Matterhorn with her mountain guide Otto Furrer. During the descent over the Italian Ridge a fixed rope broke and both of them fell. The woman was seriously injured; for the mountain guide, however, help came too late.

When Mrs. Erlanger was in Zermatt in 1961 again, she arranged with the then caretaker of the Hörnli Hut, Matthäus Kronig, to set up a Madonna at the foot of the climb of the Matterhorn. The Mother of God with the holy child was to be a gift to the mountain guides of Zermatt. Hans von Matt, a sculptor from Stans, was given the contract to create a memorial stone with the Madonna.

After von Matt had made a plaster mould, it was cast in bronze. On 27th July of the year 1962, Matthäus Kronig was working on a niche for the Madonna to stand in. On the evening of the same day at supper he died of a heart attack. The Madonna was set up next to his bier and later inserted into the niche.

In 1981 the Madonna was lost. For a long time it was thought to have been taken away by souvenir hunters. Thereupon the society of mountain guides of Zermatt decided to set a new Madonna up at the foot of the climb. A six foot-high bronze statue weighing 460 kg was made by a church sculptor, Joseph Rickenbacher from Central Switzerland.

At the beginning of July 1983 the seated Madonna with her child in her arms was screwed fast into a hollow 23 feet above the foot of the climb. On Sunday 10th July, the new Madonna was consecrated by the local clergyman, the Reverend Imhof. It was only thanks to generous donations that such a beautiful and large statue was able to be made. When the German Benedikt Pfister was finding out his way to the beginning of the Zmutt Ridge on 11th August 1989, he caught sight of something glittering on the glacier. On taking a closer look, it turned out to be the old Madonna at the base. The commemorative stone had probably been lifted out of the hollow by ice and thrown onto the glacier. Eight years later the glacier released the Madonna again.

The next day the German was struck and injured by a rock fall on the Zmutt Ridge. In hospital one finger had to be amputated. Miraculously, his life could be saved.
Today the old Madonna of the Matterhorn can be seen in the local library of Zermatt.

The Chapel at the Schwarzsee

If you walk past the Schwarzsee to the Hörnli Hut, you will see a small lake below the path, next to which stands a white chapel. It is consecrated to Mother Maria of the Snow. As to the year of its construction, no documents exist; probably it was built in the first half of the 18th century.

An old legend tells about the origin of the chapel at the Schwarzsee:

Two men from Zermatt once wanted to return from Aosta over the Theodul Pass to their native village. On the Theodul Glacier the heavy laden men were suddenly plunged into mist and they completely lost their sense of direction. Faced with violent winds and snow flurries, they were on the verge of despair. Exhausted from the long walk, they gave up hope of being rescued and promised that, if they found their way again, they would have a house of prayer built on that spot. Soon after the mist lifted and the two men from Zermatt spotted a Maria shrine near the Schwarzsee. There they had the house of worship built.

In 1784 the bishop from Sion, Franz Melchior Zenruffinen, had the house of worship pronounced a chapel for public mass. In times of drought the people would pilgrimage to the chapel at the Schwarzsee in order to ask the Holy Mother for rain.

In the years from 1980—1982 the chapel was made to look its best again by the restorer Artho and Walter Furrer from Brig under the auspices of the Society for the Protection of Ancient Monuments. On 5th August 1982 the ceremonial inauguration of the renovated chapel took place.

Even today many mountain climbers visit the chapel at the Schwarzsee in order to ask for Mary's protection during their next ascent. Every year on the 5th August, the inhabitants of Zermatt hold a grand celebration at the chapel.

The Mountain Huts on the Matterhorn

Probably only few mountains in the world have as many huts built on them as the Matterhorn. Many of these refuges have a long tale of woe to tell. In the last century one hut after another fell into ruins and other lodgings were installed elsewhere. The following is the history of the mountain huts on the Matterhorn.

The Hut on the Cravatte

Two years after the first ascent of the Matterhorn the first hut on the mountain was built under the supervision of Jean-Antoine Carrel. The Bivouac offered space enough for five to six people and was situated at 13,490 feet on the Lion Ridge on a strip of snow (called Cravatte) below the Pic Tyndall. Actually, a large hut was planned here, but due to disagreements between the banks, a large part of the collected money went astray.

For more than a decade this hut was the starting-point for the ascent of the Matterhorn on the Italian side. This bivouac fell to pieces in time because it was neglected.

The Upper Matterhorn Hut (Old Hut)

On the side of Zermatt, too, things were being organised. One year later, in 1868, on the initiative of Alexander Seiler, and with the help of the Swiss Alpine Club, Section Monte Rosa, a small hut was constructed on the Hörnli Ridge at the altitude of 12,500 feet. The brothers Knubel from St. Niklaus supervised the project.

It was a small wooden construction, protected by dry stone walls, and it provided for seven to eight persons. From year to year the disorder in this hut increased. In 1884 a few mountaineers burnt the door of this hut and a little later the wind swept away the roof of the refuge. Owing to a split in the rock, the remaining parts of the hut, including the foundations, were torn down into the depths. Today all that is left is an old wooden board.

The Stokje Hut

In the year 1875 another hut was built. It stood in a small recess of rock between the Tiefmatten Glacier and the Zmutt Glacier. At that time, with 36 bunks, it was the biggest Matterhorn hut. The Stokje Hut was the starting-point for climbing the Zmutt Ridge of the Matterhorn.
This hut also fell into ruins, and an avalanche put the definite end to its existence in November 1889. Although there were plans, it was never rebuilt.

The Hörnli Hut

Following the suggestion of the hotel manager Alexander Seiler, the decision was made to erect a hut at 10,700 feet on the Zermatt side at the foot of the climb of the Hörnli Ridge.
In September 1880 the simple stone hut with «dry walls» was accomplished.
From this point most of the ascents of the Matterhorn began.
But unfortunately the hut was often left dirty and in disorder. At the end of the last century the hut was partly repaired. In 1902 the Section Monte Rosa of the Swiss Alpine Club took over the hut. But not until 1915 was it back in perfect condition after a thorough transformation and enlargement. The hut could, as arranged with the community of Zermatt, take 17 people under its roof.
At the end of the fifties and at the beginning of the sixties the Hörnli Hut was not able to keep up with the great rush for the Matterhorn. It was pulled down at the end of 1964 and rebuilt in the following year. Since then it can put up 51 mountaineers in two dormitories.

The Gran-Torre Hut

The second hut on the Lion Ridge was built at an altitude of 12,760 ft. in 1885 by the Section Aosta of the Italian Alpine Club at the great «Tower» (Grande Torre). This small shelter measured 134 square feet and offered accomodation for ten people.

Only a few years later a better and larger hut was built a little lower down. This is why the Gran-Torre Hut was given up and left unattended.

The Capanna Luigi Amedeo di Savoia

In 1893 the Section Torino of the Italian Alpine Club constructed a new hut at the great «Tower». This hut cost them 5640 lire and was intended for ten persons. It stands on a narrow crest on the Italian side of the Matterhorn. In the sixties it could not cope with the run on the mountain. Therefore another, new hut was erected only a few feet away. Today the Capanna Luigi Amedeo di Savoia is used only when the Capanna J.A. Carrel is booked up.

The Hotel Belvédère

In the years from 1909—1911, the community of Zermatt had the Hotel Belvédère built next to the Hörnli Hut. The hotel had 20 rooms and 40 beds. It came to 100,000 sfr., including the construction of a road from the Schwarzsee to the Belvédère.

In 1923 the Hotel Bevédère and the Hörnli Hut were connected to the telephone network and this was put into service in 1924.

During the years 1980—1985 the Hotel Belvédère was renovated step by step.

The Solvay Hut

The highest hut on the Matterhorn today lies at 13,130 feet on the Hörnli Ridge.

When the number of accidents on the Matterhorn started increasing at the end of the last century, the demand came for a hut at a higher altitude. Long negotiations were necessary before the construction of this hut could be started in the second year of the First World War. The building materials had to be transported by mules via the Schwarzsee to the Hörnli Hut. A small cable car was installed, from which the material could be carried up to 13,120 feet above sea-level. Under the leadership of Oskar Supersaxo the workmen set to work on the hut on 27th August 1915. Only five days later the 82 foot-long, 12 foot-wide and 15 foot-high emergency shelter was finished. This emergency accommodation is dedicated to the Belgian industrialist Ernest Solvay, as he had financed the project. Owing to bad weather the hut was not able to be inaugurated until two years later, on 8th August 1917.

In 1966 the Solvay Hut was renovated and in 1976 the first emergency radio equipment was installed, which was worked by solar energy. The Solvay Hut is an emergency shelter and therefore must only be used in urgent situations.

Rifugio Duca degli Abruzzi (Rifugio dell'Oriondé)

The private mountain guesthouse «Duca degli Abruzzi» is situated below the South Face at an altitude of 9,200 feet. It was erected in 1929 by the Maquignaz family of Cervinia. This hut, which provides for 40 people, is used mainly by mountaineers envisaging an ascent of the South Face. The mountain guesthouse is not so frequently occupied by climbers of the Italian Ridge, as it lies a good deal lower than the other huts on the ridge and because an earth road leads to it. But many a climber of the Matterhorn has been glad to take a rest there after a long mountain tour.

The construction of the Solvay Hut 1915

(photographs: Archives of the Swiss Alpine Museum, Berne)

The Capanna K2

In 1954 the Cervino Co., (operators of the cable cars in Cervinia, domiciled in Turin) spent four million lire on a new hut called «K2», which is the name of the world's second highest mountain. It is situated on the moraine below the South Face. The hut was inaugurated in 1955. But its days were numbered; an avalanche destroyed it on 1st January 1969. Some of its ruins can still be seen on the moraine.

The Capanna Jean-Antoine Carrel

As the amount of space provided by the Capanna Luigi Amedeo di Savoia left much to be desired, a new hut was built 16.5 feet lower on the same ridge. Today it is the starting-point for ascents via the Lion Ridge. The Capanna Jean-Antoine Carrel has accommodation for 40 people and cooking facilities; there is, however, no warden.

The Oreste Bossi Bivouac

The last shelter to be set up was the Oreste Bossi Bivouac, namely in 1969, 330 feet to the north-west of the Breuil Joch. The bivouac is situated at an altitude of 10,970 feet, can put up nine people and serves as the starting-point of the Furggen Ridge.

In this list the Schönbiel Hut (1909) has been omitted because it is not considered an actual Matterhorn hut. Earlier on, the ascents of the Zmutt Ridge began at the Schönbiel Hut; nowadays, however this Ridge is usually commenced from the Hörnli Hut.

The Hotel Belvédère (left) and the Hörnli Hut

A Road up the Matterhorn

The first project for the opening up of the Matterhorn was presented to the press in the autumn of 1859 by Franz Venetz, at that time a cantonal engineer. In those days the Matterhorn was thought to be inaccessible. A 35 mile-long road from Zermatt to the foot of the Matterhorn was to be built. From here a gallery would have led inside the mountain and then a tunnel like spiral staircase would have continued to the summit.
The tunnel would have been 19—23 miles long, 5 feet wide and 8 feet high. With a maximal gradient of 10% this would have turned out to be an extraordinary path inside one of the world's most beautiful mountains. In order to be able to wonder at the breath-taking precipices on each face, numerous windows were planned. As a walking excursion at this altitude is extremely strenuous, the engineers planned resting areas at regular distances. The cost of this project was estimated at 1,250,000 Swiss francs.
Another solution, namely a continuation of the road on the sunside of the Matterhorn up to the summit was dropped, as the weather conditions were too unpredictable.
The whole idea was soon forgotten about. It is indeed astonishing to think how man's ambition might have destroyed such a beautiful mountain.

A Railway up the Matterhorn

At the end of June 1892, the engineer Xaver Imfeld from Obwalden and the heirs of L. Heer-Bétrix from Bienne received permission from the Federal Council for the construction of a railway up to the Gornergrat and the Matterhorn.

Imfeld's project for the Matterhorn included a cable car to the Schwarzsee. The next stage would have been a rack and pinion railway, protected by a series of galleries which would have been built up to the foot of the mountain. After this partially underground section, the connection for the last stage would have had its starting-point here. Inside the mountain a funicular would have led up to the summit. This railway would have been more than three miles long and would have had a gradient of more than 75%.

This project for many million francs would have had its end-station about 60 feet below the summit of the Matterhorn. From there the passengers would have left the tunnel and walked up to the summit on a well-built footpath, equipped with a safety fence. Thus, anybody would have been able to stroll about between the Swiss and the Italian summits, marvelling at the panoramic view.

Of course the inevitable grand restaurant and souvenir shop would have had their place! At that time the fare up the Matterhorn would have amounted to about 50—60 Swiss francs.

Fortunately only the railway up to the Gornergrat was realized at the end of the last century, and the permit for the Matterhorn project expired. Yet in 1907 Imfeld produced a new idea. He wanted to carry out a similar project for which he also managed to obtain a license. The Swiss and English protested loudly against this plan which would definitely have caused serious damage to the countryside. Ernest Bovet from Basel, authorised representative of the Nature Conservation Society and professor at the Federal College of Technology, launched a petition against the planned railway. Only thanks to this determined intervention could the dignity of the Matterhorn be saved, and this crazy project was forgotten about.

Approximately 50 years later, when the Italians had a cable car built to Furggen (between the Matterhorn and the Theodul Pass), strong objections were voiced by mountain lovers. Rumours spread that the engineer, Count Lora Totina from Turin, was considering a continuation of the Furggen railway up to the Matterhorn. In due course over 114,000 signatures were collected and sent to the government in Rome. Once again a big mischief on the Matterhorn was successfully avoided and so the mountain escaped total devastation. One hopes that our descendants will have more understanding and will not entertain ideas of this sort.

The Illumination of the Matterhorn

Even now the Matterhorn is in no way safe from projects. The most recent example, presented to the press in 1988, was the proposal to illuminate the mountain. For the occasion of the 700th anniversary of the Swiss Confederation (1991), the engineer Herbert Schöttl intended to turn the Matterhorn into a shining mountain.

On the three ridges, the Furggen Ridge, the Hörnli Ridge and the Zmutt Ridge, the engineer had plans to install a wire rope. Parallel to it, an electric cable would have been laid. Every 100 feet supports would have been cemented into the rock and lamps affixed. The whole undertaking would have cost a cool four million Swiss francs.

What a humiliation for such a majestic mountain! Luckily the local authority, as well as the tourist board of Zermatt, were firmly opposed to this idea. Probably the Matterhorn would have been climbed day and night and the mountain rescue team would have had even more to do recovering the injured and the dead. As if there were not already enough foolhardy mountaineers who risk their lives in the daytime.

In 1989 Schöttl once again presented his project to illuminate the Matterhorn in a modified version to the Federal council. This time, in order to avoid damage to the mountain, he intended to illuminate the Matterhorn by laser light. At the beginning of 1990 the Local Assembly of Zermatt voiced a definite refusal to such a project.

The idea of illuminating the Matterhorn, however is not new. In fact, the «King of the Mountains» was already once illuminated in 1965 from Italy. Let's hope that in future the Matterhorn will be spared such projects.

The Formation of the Matterhorn

Two different legends are told about the origins of the Matterhorn:

1. Once more God was wandering through the world; over hedge and ditch He moved in order to observe and examine His work of creation. So one fine day He came to the wild Alpine world around Zermatt. As He was crossing a mountain pass (today called Theodul Pass), His walking stick suddenly got stuck in the rock. Pulling and tugging did not help. The stick refused to budge. As He wrenched at the stick again with all His might, the upper part broke off. The point, however, was firmly anchored in the stone and could not be dislodged. Since that day the broken-off part of God's stick is called the Matterhorn.

2. Many thousands of years ago a giant whose name was Gargantua lived in the valley of Valtournanche. The sunny valley was protected from the cold North Wind by a high wall of rocks. So, in this valley Nature was able to flourish unhindered. This part of the world was very fertile. Even milk flowed in little streams, from which the small lambs drank.
The giant was well-disposed towards the dwellers of this valley. However, one day he felt he absolutely must have a look over the wall of rocks. As he touched Zermatt with his foot, the whole wall tumbled down. Only the Matterhorn was left towering over this mass of ruins.
From that day on, a north wind blows unimpeded down to the valley. Glaciers have formed and the snow lies on the fields more than six months of the year.

Actually, this second legend comes very close to the truth about the formation of the Matterhorn. In more than a hundred million years erosion carried away rock masses from the then rising mountains both southwards and northwards. Between Zermatt and Valtournanche only one larger, insignificant pyramid managed to resist this process. This pyramid was sculpted by

glaciers, wind and water, so that the magnificent shape of to-day's Matterhorn was formed.
However, wind and weather are still at work on the Matterhorn. And so the Matterhorn is merely a transient apparition like everything else in this world.

Part IV

THE MATTERHORN ADVENTURE

Photographic Aspects

The first entire panoramic view from the summit was made by Vittorio Sella on 29th July 1882. The Italian then composed the view out of single pictures measuring 20 by 24 cm. He is considered one of the pioneers of Alpine photography.

* * *

In 1901 the first film of an ascent of the Matterhorn was made.

Gliders and Helicopters

The Bernese glider pilot Alwin Kuhn was the first to circle the Matterhorn with a glider on 24th July 1946. He had taken off at midday from the Riffelberg, crossed the valley of Zermatt and then gained altitude near the slopes of the Obergabelhorn. Then he flew between the Matterhorn and the Dent d' Hérens over the Col de Tournanche on to the Col du Lion where he again found a strong thermic lift. Thanks to this he managed to glide round the Matterhorn at the height of the Solvay Hut. Soon after he landed safe and sound in Zermatt. His flight had lasted 3½ hours and he had gained more than 5,000 feet height from the Riffelberg.

* * *

On a Saturday morning in July 1966, Bruno Bagnoud, a pilot of the rescue service, flew his helicopter onto the summit of the Matterhorn. For the first time in history this pilot alighted his Alouette III on the approximately 65 foot-long and 6½ foot-wide summit ridge with the rotor blades turning, taking off again shortly after.

With this experiment he intended to enlarge his experience for particularly problematic rescue operations in the mountains. Therefore it is understandable that Bagnoud refused to repeat this performance just for the sake of a tourist.

Amazing

At the end of the last century a blind alpinist scaled the Matterhorn, accompanied by guides. A blind Swede, however, was not fortunate enough to find a guide willing to undertake an ascent of the Matterhorn with him.

* * *

The famous mountaineer Geoffrey Winthrop Young, who had had some brilliant achievements in Zermatt, was wounded so badly in the First World War, that his leg had to be taken off. In 1928 Young was in Zermatt again. He had practised a great deal with his wooden leg and once again wanted to undertake bigger challenges. Already having scaled the Monte Rosa the year before, he now tackled the Wellenkuppe, the Weisshorn and finally the Matterhorn. He started out with Hans Brantschen and another guide at ten p.m. from the Hotel Belvédère and reached the top of the Matterhorn after 9½ hours' strenuous ascent.

In 1948 a one-legged Austrian arrived at the top on crutches together with some friends. In the fifties a one-legged sportsman was seen even on the Zmutt Ridge.

The mountain guide from Zermatt Oswald Julen told the story of an ascent he made with one of his guests. On the way down the guest wished to take a long rest at the Solvay Hut. When the mountain guide entered the hut a little later, he saw, much to his surprise, that his guest was screwing off his leg. Julen hadn't noticed that his guest was wearing an artificial leg.
Not often in his life had the mountain guide Eddy Petrig been so moved as when he stood on the top of the Matterhorn in 1974

with the Englishman Norman Croucher and the aspiring mountain guide Leo Imesch. The Englishman had lost both his legs from the knees down when he had been run over by a train. All the same Croucher had climbed the mountain in the admirable time of seven hours, and this although it had snowed two inches during the night.

Cold Nights

On 24th December 1936, the Italian Giusto Gervasutti climbed up the Matterhorn alone, taking the route over the Lion Ridge in extreme wintry conditions. He spent Christmas Eve there in his sleeping bag. Gervasutti was the first to have climbed this ridge alone in winter.

Since then some few alpinists have bivouacked on the summit of the mountain, among them René Arnold from Zermatt. The mountain lovers mostly spent the night on this spot in order to admire the sunset and sunrise.

A German couple wanted to spend their wedding night on the summit of the Matterhorn. But the newly marrieds fell to their death during the ascent.

Round the Mountain

On 25th September 1941 Luigi Carrel, Pierre Maquignaz and Albert Deffeyes went up via the Hörnli Ridge to an altitude of 14,100 ft. From there they crossed the East Face and after 90 minutes reached the Furggen Shoulder. Then they traversed the South Face, the West Face via the Carrel-Gallery and the North Face. At three o' clock in the afternoon they were on the Hörnli Ridge again and climbed up to the summit.

Thus they had climbed round the Matterhorn at lofty heights.

All Four Ridges

The mountain guides René Arnold and Sepp Graven from Zermatt challenged all four ridges of the Matterhorn in one day on 28th September 1966. At 1.30 a.m. the men left their bivouac at the foot of the climb of the Furggen Ridge in order to scale this most difficult ridge of the mountain. After having gone round the overhangs from the south, they reached the summit at 7.30 a.m. and after a fifteen-minute rest they descended via the Hörnli Ridge to the Hörnli Hut, which they entered at 9.30 a.m.
At 10.30, after a substantial meal, they traversed the Matterhorn Glacier and approached the summit via the Zmutt Ridge. Only 8½ hours had gone by since they had stood on the top the previous time.
The descent took place half-an-hour later via the Lion Ridge. The mountain guides were taken by surprise by clouds and damp mist at the level of the Tyndall Rope (name of a place on the Lion Ridge). Now they had to proceed with the utmost caution, as the rocks were covered with ice and hoar frost. At 9 p.m. the two natives of Zermatt arrived at the little village of Breuil after a successful expedition.

In Old Age

The oldest climber of the Matterhorn is Ulrich Inderbinen. For the special event of the 125th anniversary of the first ascent of the Matterhorn (14th July 1990) the mountain guide of Zermatt, Ulrich Inderbinen, climbed the Matterhorn via the Hörnli Ridge at the age of 90 years with a colleague mountain guide. With this, the ninety-year-old indeed performed an astonishing masterpiece. Quite rightly, Ulrich Inderbinen was proclaimed the «King of the Matterhorn» by a journalist.
The oldest climber of the Italian Ridge is Jacopo Linussio from Udine. At the age of 85 he reached the summit of the Matterhorn in the autumn of 1989.

Adventures of Mountain Guides

On 9th August 1950 the Zermatt mountain guide Edmund Biner was heading from the Hörnli Hut towards the foot of the climb of the Matterhorn, when a black and white cat followed him. She belonged to the cook of the hut, Josephine Aufdenblatten. The weather conditions on the mountain were bad; new snow had fallen. At first the cat remained at the foot of the climb. In the evening the cook noticed that her cat was missing. The next day the weather was good. As a lot of people wanted to go up the Matterhorn, the mountain guides set out earlier than usual on that day. Shortly before the mountain guide August Julen reached the ridge (about 12,130 ft.), he heard the mewing of a cat. It was Josephine Aufdenblatten's pet. A little further down Edmund Biner was climbing up. At first the cat followed the two mountain guides and their guests. At the level of the lower Mosley Slab she took a different way from the men and came to the Solvay Hut. There the guides gave her some food.

After a short break the cat followed the roped parties on the left side of the upper Mosley Slab. The cat tried hard to hold on to the fixed ropes with her claws, but it was no good. The mountain guides didn't think the cat would follow them any higher. But the animal overcame these difficulties and reached the middle of the crest. At this point the snow had been blown away and the surface was slippery.

All of a sudden the cat slid down several feet, until she was able to save herself by gripping a ledge in the rock. Then the animal managed to get up to the summit. Biner went over the summit in order to descend via the Italian Ridge. Julen, on the other hand, wanted to feed the cat and take her in his rucksack, but the little animal ran away.

Later on, an Italian guide took her with him down to Italy. Although the Italians were asked to bring the cat back to the cook, they kept the animal in Breuil. The following winter Edmund Biner found the cat again. She had been stuffed and was standing in a restaurant in Breuil.

Only three years later some mountain guides discovered a cat on the Zmutt Ridge. The poor animal, whose paws were battered and torn, was packed into a rucksack and brought safely down to the valley.

But she was not to be the last animal on the mountain. Many years later a German carried his dachshund up the Matterhorn in his rucksack. Occasionally mountain goats have been spotted on the Matterhorn.

* * *

In the fifties August Julen climbed the Matterhorn with an American woman. All the time during the ascent the woman from the United States complained that she felt too hot. On the way down she continued to grumble and stripped off one garment after the other, till she arrived at the Solvay Hut wearing nothing but a bra on her top half. While she was climbing down over the lower Mosley Slab, her bra got hooked up on a rock and the skimpy garment tore.

* * *

In the seventies Leo Imesch, a mountain guide from Zermatt, ascended the Matterhorn with a guest in good time. After a few of those inevitable photos on the summit, the Englishman asked his guide, «are you allowed to play golf up here?» The guide answered, «I should think so». Upon this, the Englishman took out of his rucksack the end of a golf club, a spiral ice-screw and two balls. By screwing the spiral ice-screw together with the head of the golf club, the mountaineer had made himself a one foot-long golf club. With this, the Englishman hit two balls from the summit; one in the direction of Italy and one in the direction of Switzerland. These were to be his greetings to the fellow members of his golf club.

* * *

In 1988 a mountain guide called Hugo Biner was on the Matterhorn with an American guest. The conditions on the mountain could not have been better and a lot of people were heading eagerly towards the summit.

At the second couloir the American lost the sole of one of his mountain boots. The mountain guide had him put a crampon on and went on. When they came to the third couloir the man from the U.S.A. lost the other shoe sole. Once again he had to put on a crampon. In the meantime they had been overtaken by several roped parties. With any other guest, Hugo Biner would have turned back; but, as the American was celebrating his 40th birthday that day, he decided to carry on.

So the American still managed to reach the top of the mountain on the day of his birthday. In the evening the man was exhausted, as he had had to walk all the way down with crampons on his feet.

It is rumoured that some tourists have fixed their crampons on the wrong way round (the spikes facing backwards) or even put their mountain boots on the wrong way round.

The Musicians

The French violinist André de Ribeaupierre took his violin with him up onto the summit and there he played Johann Sebastian Bach's «Chaconne».

* * *

On 15th August 1986, Walter Gruber and Odilo Summermatter from St. Niklaus in the Valais, together with some friends, were on the Matterhorn with a somewhat unusual load. They had been obliged to turn back on the Hörnli Ridge in July, but this time the weather seemed to be favourable. Concealed in their rucksacks were objects wrapped in cloths; but their secret was not to be revealed until they were at the highest point.

When the group of mountaineers had reached the top at 9 a.m., they unpacked the precious load. The separate parts of two alphorns appeared one after another and were put together. Then the two alphorn players gave a performance at a height of 14,687 ft.

Art

In mid-September 1987 the local artist Heinz Julen had a 30 foot-high piece of sculpture which weighed 200 kg flown up onto the Matterhorn. The colourful piece of sculpture, which was run by solar energy, was set up near the Cross on the summit. Even the Swiss Television was not to be left out of this short but extraordinary presentation.

Publicity

For publicity reasons two 200 kg boulders were transported from the peak of the Matterhorn to the ski-resorts of Snowbird and Vail in America.

In order to heal the wound on the mountain, the sculptor André Bucher from Obwalden (at the time living in Geneva) made a rock-shaped replacement out of bronze and had it flown from Geneva up to the summit by two helicopters in the summer of 1986. With the help of a winch the replacement rock was lowered onto the correct spot.

By doing this he wanted to protest against the commercial exploitation of the mountain. The replacement piece, weighing 70 kg, had to be removed again at the request of the local authority of Zermatt.

This was not the first time that a piece of the Matterhorn's peak was removed. In 1868 François Thioly from Geneva took a piece of rock from the highest point of the mountain with him. This rock is supposed to have been on sale for 5,50 Swiss francs in the forties of this century. Before the First World War yet another stone was dug out from the summit under legal supervision. This piece of the summit was fowarded to a museum in Berlin. But the stone was lost in an allied bombing raid.

In 1983 four mountaineers carried a 1,650 kg-heavy boulder down from the Matterhorn.

In 1986 a Swiss importer of a Japanese camera factory had a camera, made to the scale of 8:1, flown onto the Matterhorn on the occasion of the 25th anniversary of his business. The plywood camera weighed 100 kg, was 4 feet long, and was erected next to the Solvay Hut. There every mountaineer was able to have his picture taken just by pressing a button. The local authority of Zermatt ordered the immediate removal of the camera.

Jokes

In September 1987 the entertainer Kurt Felix of the German Television Company (ARD) had a newspaper kiosk flown onto the Matterhorn and set in the face beneath the Solvay Hut. Felix intended to fox the world-famous mountaineer Reinhold Messner with a «candid camera». Reinhold Messner was climbing the Matterhorn early in the morning, when to his indignation he found a newspaper kiosk there selling the latest international papers. Even his own book was offered to him by the famous ski acrobat Art Furrer. After the successfull joke Felix had the newspaper kiosk removed straight away.

Irresponsible . . .

There are always people to whom life seems boring. They have to prove themselves or they want to appear in the newspaper. What would be more appropriate than some dare-devilry on the mountain of the mountains?
As the following examples show, such dare-devil actions are to be compared with Russian roulette. The following account is not meant to encourage young people to rash new adventures, but to inspire a sense of respect. Many a man has had to pay for his Matterhorn project with his life. As if there had not already been enough tragic accidents on this mountain!
Foolhardiness and lack of common sense rarely pay in this way. The rescue service of Zermatt sets out dozens of times every year

in order to rescue victims on the Matterhorn. Most of them are written about in the newspapers, but too often, alas, their names are followed by a black cross.

One day in September of the year 1984, two Germans arrived at the Hörnli Hut. They were only wearing track suits and anoraks. And yet: the Germans wanted to ascend the Matterhorn! Their goal was to jog up the mountain. Contrary to all common sense they went to the Matterhorn the nexy day. Still a long way away from the summit they had to give up.
Frightening minutes passed until they were fetched by a helicopter. They have never, however, been able to set foot on the summit.

* * *

In the summer of 1966 two Austrians had themselves flown with a helicopter to the altitude of 16,400 ft. near the Matterhorn. From this altitude Erich Felbermayr and Walter Leindecker jumped out with their parachutes parallel to the North Face of the Matterhorn. The parachutes opened up and both men landed safe and sound at the foot of the climb.
Even more daring was the Frenchman Pierre Gevaux. In 1984 he climbed the Matterhorn. On the summit he hacked out a small runway in the snow. As soon as the wind conditions were favourable, he took his run up with crampons on his feet and flung himself into the emptyness by the North Face. Once he had got plenty of distance from the face, he opened his parachute and landed less than ten minutes later at the Schwarzsee.

* * *

In August 1977 three mountaineers climbed up the Matterhorn heavily loaded. In their luggage there were three hang-gliders, each of them weighing 14 kg. On the summit the three set up their flying machines and prepared for the take-off. The first to fly was Zino Diemer from Munich. Shortly afterwards, Diemer had disappeared in the mist, and his two friends Karl Aichholzer and Peter Altenhofer from Austria took off. In twenty minutes the

Austrians glided from the summit to Winkelmatten. After the landing the two aviators missed their German friend. Diemer had had to pay for this dare-devil undertaking with his life. Eyewitnesses thought at first that a helicopter had crashed into the North Face, but it had been the hang-glider of the German.

Marcel Lachat from Geneva was the first Swiss to repeat such a mad attempt.

Jean-Marc Boivin also flew down from the Matterhorn with a hang-glider. Strong winds on 5th August 1981 made the plan difficult to carry out.

Boivin landed at the base of the North Face, packed up his hang-glider and climbed up this Face on the same day to the summit.

* * *

The first to challenge the mountain on skis was Toni Valeruz from South Tyrol. In May 1975 he climbed nine hours up to the shoulder of the Hörnli Ridge. From there the ski-instructor skied into the East Face of the Matterhorn. The run lasted 21 minutes and 45 seconds. Mist and rock-fall turned this challenge into a matter of life and death. Valeruz had taken two years to prepare for this run and had developed a special jumping technique.

The next dare-devil was Jean-Marc Boivin. In 1981, on 8th June, Boivin bivouacked on the summit of the Matterhorn. The next morning the Frenchman descended on foot to an altitude of 13,950 ft., put on his skis and skied down the East Face.

Four years later Yoshimasa Wada tried it. Belayed by two mountain guides, the Japanese slid down the crest, or, to be exact, was hoisted down. Not until the lowest part of the East Face was Wada on his own and skiing down without being secured by a rope. For the first time a skier had «skied» down from the peak; not, however, without help.

In mid-July 1977 an American wanted to ski down the North Face of the Matterhorn. But he fell during the climb up on the fixed ropes. Only his helmet and a few of his skull bones were found. His body was probably swallowed by a crevasse in the glacier.

On 15th June 1989, the ski-instructor André Anzévui from the Valais had himself flown onto the Matterhorn. The first couple of feet of the mountain he covered on his skis. After this he used the fixed ropes on the crest in order to get lower. He skied a short stretch over the shoulder, was then picked up by a helicopter and set down on the icy flank of the North Face, from where he mastered the 60 degrees-steep strip of ice on skis again.

* * *

On 22nd August 1987 Bruno Gouvy from Chamonix was flown from Italy onto the summit. He descended to the Solvay Hut on foot in order to ski for two hours on the snow-laden East Face with his surf ski. In the middle of the face he once had to abseil. With this, in one single day, he had skied down the Eiger, the Grandes Jorasses and the Matterhorn on the surf ski.

THE CHRONICLES OF THE MATTERHORN

Owing to its importance, the North Face is listed separately in this account.

1857   1st attempt on the ascent by J.A. Carrel, J.J. Carrel and Aimé Gorret on the Lion Ridge up to 12,211 ft. (3723 m)

        2nd attempt by V. Carrel and G. Maquignaz on the Lion Ridge up to 11,316 ft. (3450 m)

1858   3rd attempt by J.A. Carrel and J.J. Carrel on the Lion Ridge up to 12,464 ft. (3800 m)

1860   4th attempt by the brothers A., C. and S. Parker on the Hörnli Ridge up to 11,808 ft. (3600 m)

        5th attempt by J. Tyndall, J.J. Bennen, E.V. Hawkins and J.J. Carrel on the Lion Ridge up to 12,988 ft. (3960 m)

1861   6th attempt by the brothers Parker on the Hörnli Ridge up to 12,136 ft. (3700 m)

        7th attempt by J.A. Carrel and J.J. Carrel on the Lion Ridge up to 13,224 ft. (4032 m)

        8th attempt by E. Whymper with a guide from the Bernese Oberland on the Lion Ridge up to 12,644 ft. (3855 m)

1862   9th attempt (in January) by T.S. Kennedy with the Guides P. Perren and P. Taugwalder senior on the Hörnli Ridge up to 11,152 ft. (3400 m)

        10th attempt by E. Whymper, R. Macdonald, L. Meynet with J. Zumtaugwald and J. Kronig on the Lion Ridge up to 11,994 ft. (3657 m)

        11th attempt by E. Whymper, R. Macdonald, J.A. Carrel and Pession on the Lion Ridge up to 12,988 ft. (3960 m)

        12th attempt by E. Whymper on his own on the Lion Ridge up to 13,395 ft. (4084 m). Whymper falls, escapes with slight injuries.

13th attempt by E. Whymper, J.A. Carrel, C. Carrel and L. Meynet on the Lion Ridge up to 13,120 ft. (4000 m)

14th attempt by E. Whymper and L. Meynet on the Lion Ridge up to 13,454 ft. (4102 m)

15th attempt by J. Tyndall with the 4 guides J.J. Bennen, A. Walter, J.A. Carrel and C. Carrel on the Lion Ridge up to 13,966 ft. (4258 m) (Pic Tyndall)

1863   16th attempt by E. Whymper, J.A. Carrel, C. Carrel and L. Meynet on the Lion Ridge up to 13,274 ft. (4047 m)

1865   17th attempt by E. Whymper, M. Croz, C. Almer, F. Biner and L. Meynet in the Furggen Couloir up to 11,197 ft. (3414 m)

18th attempt by J.A. Carrel, C. Carrel, C.E. Gorret and J. Maquignaz on the Lion Ridge

First ascent on 14th July by the guides from Zermatt, Peter Taugwalder senior and junior, the guide from Chamonix Michel Croz and the Englishmen, E. Whymper, C. Hudson, D. Hadow and Lord Douglas via the Hörnli Ridge. During the descent the last three Englishmen and M. Croz lose their lives.

On 17th July the summit is reached for the first time via the Lion Ridge by J.A. Carrel and J.B. Bich

1867   The first woman is on the mountain: Félicité Carrel reaches the altitude of 14,366 ft. (4380 m) on the Lion Ridge (Col Félicité)

1868   For the first time the mountain is climbed from one side and descended on the other by J. Tyndall and D. Maquignaz (Lion Ridge—Hörnli Ridge)

1871   On 22nd July the Englishwoman Lucy Walker is the first woman to set foot on the summit

1879   The Zmutt Ridge is scaled for the first time by A.F. Mummery, A. Burgener, J. Petrus and A. Gentinetta for the first time W. Penhall, F. Imseng and L. Zurbriggen climb a good part of the West Face via the Penhall Couloir

1911   The last ridge, the Furggen Ridge is ascended by J.J. Carrel, J. Gaspard and M. Piacenza by avoiding the overhangs

1929   F. Herrmann is the first soloclimber to scale the major part of the West Face

1931   First scaling of the South Face by L. Carrel, M. Bich and E. Benedetti

1932   Pioneering ascent of the East Face by L. Carrel, L. Carrel, E. Benedetti, M. Bich, A. Gaspard and G. Mazzotti

1933   A. Crétier, T. Gaspard and B. Olietti conquer the De-Amicis-Ridge. During the descent they are killed

1941   First complete climbing of the whole Furggen Ridge by L. Carrel, A. Perino and G. Chiara

1942   First ascent of the Deffeyes-Carrel-Ridge in the South Face by L. Carrel and A. Deffeyes

1953   Opening of the Muzio-Carrel-Route by I. Muzio, L. Carrel and L. Maquignaz in the South Face

1962   First complete scaling of the West Face by G. Ottin and R. Gaguin

1963   The South South-East Face (to the Pic Muzio) is scaled for the first time by G. Lanfranconi and A. Zucchi

1969   Pioneering ascent of the Zmuttnose by L. Cerruti and A. Gogna

1970   G. Machetto, G. Calcagno, L. Cerruti and C. Di Pietro climb the southeast pillar to the Pic Muzio for the first time

1981   The direct Zmuttnose is climbed for the first time by M. Piola and P.A. Steiner

1982   First solo climb via the Gogna-Route on the Zmuttnose by A. Georges

1983   R. Casarotto and G. Grassi establish a new route in the South Face (between the De-Amicis-Ridge and the Deffeyes-Carrel-Ridge)

        A new route is laid over the South Face to the Pic Muzio by M. Barmasse and V. De Tuoni

        The «Direttissima» of the South Face is achieved for the first time by V. De Tuoni, W. Cazzanelli and M. Barmasse

The Ascents in Winter
(All successful summit ascents between 21st December and 21st March count as winter ascents! In earlier days, ascents made at the end of March or in April were also included.)

1875   1st winter ascent of the Hörnli Ridge by A. Carrel, J.P. Maquignaz, J.J.Maquignaz, L. Meynet and G. Corona

1882   V. Sella, Jean-Antoine, Louis and Baptiste Carrel climb the Lion Ridge for the first time in winter

1948   1st winter/spring ascent of the Zmutt Ridge by E. Petrig and H. Masson

        1st winter/spring ascent of the upper part of the Furggen Ridge by J. Fuchs and R. Monney

1949   1st winter/spring ascent of the greater part of the West Face by J. Fuchs and R. Monney

1953   W. Bonatti and R. Bignami do the first entire climb of the Furggen Ridge in winter

1964   For the first time the De-Amicis-Ridge is scaled in winter by L. Ratto and G. Ottin

1971   First winter climb of the South Face by A. and O. Squinobal as well as E. Bich and I. Mennabreaz (1 hour later)

1974   1st ascent in winter of the Zmuttnose by E. Oberson and T. Gross

1975   R. Arnold, G. Bumann and C. Pralonge succeed in the first ascent of the East Face in winter

1978   R. Albertini, M. Barmasse, L. Pession, A. Tamone, I. Mennabreaz, as well as the brothers A. and O. Squinobal carry out the 1st winter ascent of the West Face. During the climb down Albertini falls and is killed

1982   D. Anker and T. Wüschner master the Piola-Steiner-Route of the Zmutt-nose in winter for the first time

1983   Pioneering ascent in winter of the Deffeyes-Carrel-Ridge by Leo Pession, G. Gorret, M. Barmasse and Luigi Pession

1984   The Casarotto-Grassi-Route is climbed in winter by M. Barmasse, W. Cazzanelli and A. Tamone for the first time

1987   M. Barmasse, W. Cazzanelli and N. Corradi scale the Pic Muzio via the Machetto-Route for the first time in winter

1989   The Piacenza-Route of the Furggen Ridge is climbed for the first time in winter by G. Carrozza, A. Perron and A. Tamone

The North Face

1923   1st attempt on the North Face by A. Horeschowsky and F. Piekielko

1928   2nd attempt on the North Face by V. Imboden and K. Mooser

1930   3rd attempt on the North Face by E.R. Blanchet with the guides J. Lerjen and K. Mooser

1931   For the first time the notorious North Face is scaled on 31.7/1.8. by the brothers Franz and Toni Schmid

1935   For the first time the face is scaled without a bivouac by H. Steuri and A. Bauer

1959   First solo ascent of the face by D. Marchart

1962   1st winter ascent up to the shoulder by A. Huber, F. Huber and H. Sedlmayr

        1st entire winter scaling by H. von Allmen and P. Etter

1963   1st ascent by a woman; by N. Fajdiga with A. Mahkota

1965   In a solo ascent in winter W. Bonatti finds a new route in the west part of the face

        Y. Vaucher is the first woman to climb the whole face

1972   Opening of the Japanese route on the right hand side of the face by M. Furukawa, M. Miyagawa and Y. Okitsu

        Opening of the Czechoslovakian Route (Direttissima) by Z. Drlik, L. Horka, B. Kadlcik and V. Prokes

1978   1st winter ascent of the North Face by a woman; by A. Shigi with M. Shigi

        1st women's roped party in winter on the North Face: A. Czerwinska, I. Kesa, K. Palmowska and W. Rutkiewicz

        (1 m = 3,28 ft.)

Mountain guides from Zermatt who lost their lives on the Matterhorn:

1890   Alois Graven

1893   Johann Biner

1900   Alfons Furrer

1936   Isidor Perren

1949   Adelrich Julen

1951   Otto Furrer

1990   Hermann Perren

Mountain guides from Cervinia who died on the Matterhorn:

1890   Jean-Antoine Carrel

1933   Antonio Gaspard

1947   Agostino Pellissier

1950   Alberto Bich

1978   Rolando Albertini

Bibliography:

— Hiebeler Toni, Dunkle Wand am Matterhorn, Limpert Verlag, Frankfurt 1962

— Rey Guido, Das Matterhorn, Bergverlag R. Rother, München 1959

— Whymper Edward, Berg- und Gletscherfahrten, Westermann-Verlag, Braunschweig 1922

— Wundt Theodor von, Das Matterhorn und seine Geschichte, DöAV-Sektion, Berlin 1896

— Alpen, Zeitschrift des Schweizer Alpenklubs

— Alpine Journal, Zeitschrift des Britischen Alpenklubs

— Neue Zürcher Zeitung (NZZ), Zürich

— Walliser Bote, Brig

The south side of the Matterhorn

1) *De-Amicis-Ridge*

2) *Deffeyes-Carrel-Ridge*

3) *Direttissima on the South Face (via De Tuoni-Barmasse)*

4) *Muzio-Carrel-Route to the Pic Muzio (the Pic Muzio is at the end of the dotted line)*

5) *Direct Furggen Ridge*

Beat P. Truffer has already published other books:

The latest from Zermatt – 1960 to present

This book offers the reader important information about the climate, the development, the traffic communications and the rescue service, as well as a description of the village and the neighbourhood of Zermatt. In a short time one has a good all-round view of the most important events of the last three decades in this village of the Matterhorn.
(Also available in German and French)

ISBN 3-905097-02-8

sfr. 14.80

In April 1992 an illustrated book by Beat P. Truffer will be available. Many excellent, large sized photographs show the village and the region of Zermatt. This book is a beautiful souvenir of your visit to Zermatt.

ISBN 3-905097-08-7

These books are available in your bookshop or directly at

Aroleit-Verlag, Haus Saphir,
CH-3920 Zermatt